# IN LETTERS OF GOLD

The story of Sylvia Pankhurst
and the East London Federation of the Suffragettes
in Bow

**by Rosemary Taylor**

D1477165

**Stepney Books**

© Rosemary Taylor 1993

First Published February 1993

**ISBN 0 950 5241 82**

Published by

STEPNEY BOOKS
19 Tomlins Grove
London E3 4NX

Printed by

EXPRESSION PRINTERS
49 Corsica Street
London N5 1JT

**Illustrations:**

With grateful thanks to the following copyright holders for their permission to reproduce the illustrations listed below:

Nos. 1 (front cover), 7, 10, 18, 19, 20, 23, 24, 25, 26, 28, 29, 30, 33, 36, 37, 38, 40, 42, and 44 (back cover) - International Instituut voor Sociale Geschiedenis, Amsterdam.

Nos. 2 & 22 - the Museum of London.

Nos. 3, 6, 12, 13, 15, 16, 21, 32 - Tower Hamlets Local History Library, Bancroft Road.

No. 5 (postcard view of Bromley-by-Bow) - Philip Mernick.

The sketch of the Red Cottage on page 42 - Jennifer Taylor.

Map of Bow reproduced by kind permission of the London Borough of Tower Hamlets

The remaining 15 photographs are copyright of the author.

# CONTENTS

*The sites above can be identified on the map by the chapter numbers.*

# List of Illustrations

For Amore

# ACKNOWLEDGEMENTS

The completion and publication of this book would not have been possible without the help and encouragement of Denise Jones and Jenny Smith, whose kindness and patience in shaping the work to its present standard of professionalism I acknowledge with gratitude.

To my husband, Tom for the many hours he spent driving me around Bow whenever called upon to do so, often not at the most convenient times, and his patience in waiting until the light was "just right" for a particular photograph, I acknowledge a debt of gratitude. Michael, the "computer expert" has been responsible for the supply and maintenance of my computer system and his cheerful guidance, support and hours of talking his mother through the mysteries of computer magic have left me forever in his debt. My daughter Rosanna and her husband Albert were kindness itself during my trips to Holland, and patiently arranged my often hurried appointments with the IISG, Amsterdam. To Philip, Jo, Robin and Tonya and other members of my family who were equally patient with me, especially during the times when I just had to tell someone about my latest find, and proceeded to do so at great length, I offer my grateful thanks.

My grateful thanks to Mrs Sylvia Ayling of the Sylvia Pankhurst Society, Woodford Green, who read the first draft, and provided me with her own notes and suggestions for improving the book.

I have specially to thank Chris Lloyd and Harry Watton at the Local History Library, Bancroft Road, for their unfailing support and assistance in my research and Howard Bloch of the Stratford Local History Library, for bringing to my attention valuable material from their archives.

I am deeply grateful to Thea Duyker of the International Instituut voor Sociale Geschiedenis, Amsterdam for her kindness in allowing me access to the photographic archives, and extending me every courtesy during my often hurried visits, and to the IISG for their kind permission to publish the photographs.

My grateful thanks to Maggie Hewitt of Oxford House, who has encouraged me to expand and extend my study into the creation of an educational project, by offering her professional expertise, advice and assistance. I would also like to thank Diane Atkinson for her encouragment and support in this connection.

To Mrs Andrea Silk, who so kindly came forward with her invaluable reminiscences of the Toy Factory, and so helped to fill in a forgotten chapter in its history, I am eternally grateful.

The East London History Society have supported me in all aspects of my work and I would especially like to thank Doreen Kendall, who has so enthusiastically helped me out through the years and continues to do so as the project expands. My thanks also to John Harris, who never fails to bring to my attention vital snippets of information, which he just happens come across in the course of his own research. I wish also to thank Philip Mernick for helping to solve the mystery of the "Obelisk" and for his permission to publish the postcard from his collection.

Finally, I must thank Charlie Hagon of Burdett Photographics for his patient advice and assistance with my photographs, and for his reminiscences of life in Poplar, which brought about the chance discussion on "traffic islands" and "Obelisks", which provided the final missing piece of the puzzle. Without him this mystery might never have been solved, at least for me!

The working women of the East End were projected into the limelight of the national political stage in 1888 when Annie Besant, outraged by the appalling conditions under which the matchworkers were forced to labour, inspired them to strike for better wages and conditions. The Matchgirls of Bryant and Mays walked out on strike and into the history books. It was the first successful strike of women workers led by a woman. The women of the East End went on to create their own unique brand of militancy during the formative years of labour and socialist politics on the one hand and the feminist movement on the other. George Lansbury, MP for Bow and long-serving Councillor in Poplar, was deeply committed to the dual causes of socialism and women's rights. He challenged the nation's conscience when he resigned his seat in Parliament in October 1912, so that he could fight for re-election on the issue of women's suffrage. He was narrowly defeated, and remained out of Parliament for the next twelve years.

Annie Besant was not the first woman political activist to be drawn to the East End of London, a fertile ground for socialist reform. Eleanor Marx, daughter of Karl Marx, regularly addressed meetings of the Socialist Democratic Front at the corner of Dod Street in Poplar. She played a key role in the setting up of the Gasworkers Union, writing the constitution for Will Thorne, and forming the women's branch of the union. Amy Hicks started a campaign in 1889 among the women ropemakers, and went on to form a successful Union of Women Ropemakers.

There is ample evidence to show that women in the East End were actively campaigning for female suffrage. The Women's Suffrage Society held meetings at Stratford Town Hall, one such was reported in the Stratford Express in January 1887. Several local women who were equally active in the political sphere feature in news reports. Names such as those of Rebecca Cheetham, Minnie Baldock, Adelaide Knight and Daisy Parsons crop up again and again in the Stratford papers. As members of the Board of Guardians they worked hard to improve the quality of life of working women. Adelaide Knight, frail, disabled and married to a coloured man, faced prejudice and injustice wherever she went. She made the headlines when she was arrested along with Annie Kenny and Mrs Sparborough for attempting to meet Asquith in 1906. Daisy Parsons, one of the delegation of women who did get to meet Prime Minister Asquith in 1914, went on to become the first woman Mayor of West Ham in 1936. She was awarded the MBE in 1951. Mrs Mary Pascoe, of Bromley High Street, who supported an invalid husband and several adopted orphans, worked in the Cost Price Restaurant and later in the Women's Voluntary Service. "Aunt Polly" as she was affectionately known by her friends, always treasured her Suffragette brooch, which commemorated her imprisonment in Holloway. She worked for over 35 years with the Poplar Labour Party, until her death in April 1958.

Julia Scurr, from Limehouse, Lena Wilson and Elizabeth Crooks, wife of Will Crooks, (Poplar's first Labour Mayor) organised protest meetings and led thousands of women on marches into the West End of London. Julia Scurr had a long career as a Councillor and local Guardian, working alongside George Lansbury in Bow. She led delegations to Downing Street in 1905 and again in 1914, the latter a crucial meeting with Asquith which helped to change his views on women's suffrage. The careers of women such as Poplar councillors Jennie Mackay, Julia Scurr, Nellie Cressall, Minnie Lansbury, Susan Lawrence (elected MP for East Ham North 1923) served to highlight the paradox of women's successful participation in local politics and their

# "Deeds not Words"

exclusion from parliamentary franchise and thus the national platform.

When Annie Kenny was despatched to London in 1906 by Mrs Pankhurst with a view to setting up a London branch of the WSPU, she stayed in West Ham, in the home of Minnie Baldock, a local woman involved with the Independent Labour Party. In 1892 West Ham entered the history books when James Keir Hardie was elected as the first Independent Labour Member of Parliament for South West Ham. As a friend of the Pankhurst family and dearly loved by Sylvia who valued his opinion and advice, it can have been no coincidence that the first branch of the WSPU in London was formed in Canning Town, when Sylvia Pankhurst and Annie Kenny addressed the opening meeting. Branches soon followed in Poplar, Bow, Stepney and Limehouse. In 1907 Mrs Emmeline Pethick Lawrence, honorary treasurer, and editor of **Votes for Women** wrote to Bessie Lansbury, who had joined the WSPU in 1906, thanking her for her support and sympathy.

The WSPU found they could count on the wholehearted support of East End women at rallies, marches and demonstrations. However, the enthusiasm and willingness of working women rallying to the battle cry of the Suffragettes was viewed with increasing disfavour and misgiving by Christabel Pankhurst. In 1906 she expressed her surprise that the WSPU should be exclusively dependent upon women of the East End during rallies and marches, and while she recognised this early and crucial participation in the women's suffrage movement, she simultaneously rejected their potential role in that struggle, which she saw as being exclusive to middle class women.

Christabel's attitude was merely a reflection of the rigid class structure of Edwardian England, and it is to her sister Sylvia's great credit that she was able to cross the social divide and identify with workers' aspirations, and it was this that caused the split in the Pankhurst family.

Whilst East End women activists gave their support to the WSPU and organised their own local branches, they remained rooted in the political concerns of their local communities. In the period 1890-1904 many women in the East End came under the direct influence of labour and socialist politics on the one hand, and the feminist movement on the other. It was within this matrix that their own brand of militancy was born. This high profile of feminist activity at both local and national levels was to prove a significant factor in the political development of the East End.

# E Sylvia Pankhurst

Estelle Sylvia Pankhurst was born in Manchester on 5 May 1882 to Richard and Emmeline Pankhurst, the second of five children. She died in Ethiopa in 1960, and was given a state funeral with the highest honours that country could bestow.

The Pankhurst children grew up amidst the hurly-burly of political campaigns, as both parents sought careers in public life. Her father's death in 1897 affected Sylvia deeply, and left her with a lifelong commitment to his socialist ideals. In 1903 Emmeline Pankhurst formed theWomen's Social and Political Union in Manchester, with the intention of pressurising the Labour Party into supporting the votes for women campaign. She relied on the support of her three daughters: Christabel, who became the movement's formal leader, Sylvia and Adela.

Emmeline Pankhurst's campaign for women's suffrage, Votes for Women, made headline news as the suffragettes resorted increasingly to violence and acts of vandalism in their efforts to win equality. But thanks to the first volume of her autobiography, **The Suffragette Movement,** it is Sylvia's name that is forever associated with the suffrage movement.

In 1906 the WSPU moved its headquarters to London, where Emmeline Pankhurst began her campaign in earnest. By this time, Sylvia, a gifted artist, was coming to the end of her two year scholarship at the Royal College of Art. Gradually, the struggle for women's rights took precedence, and her talent was channelled into designing posters, banners and badges. Her outstanding ability as a painter is apparent in the few paintings and sketches that have survived. Reproductions of her work can be seen in Richard Pankhurst's book **Sylvia Pankhurst, Artist and Crusader.**

In 1912 Sylvia Pankhurst came to Bow, in East London, to work with George Lansbury, who had taken up the cause of women's suffrage. She was deeply moved by the plight of the poverty-stricken women she encountered, and against the stern advice of her mother and sister, elected to speak on behalf of the working class women. It did not take her long to realise that universal suffrage was the real answer to society's ills, and to the dismay of her family, Sylvia threw in her lot with her "mates" in the East End. From the moment she wrote "Votes for Women" in letters of gold on the front of the baker's shop in the Bow Road, the East End cast its unique spell over her. In the years leading up the First World War and right through that terrible tragedy, she was to commit herself to the dual causes of peace and adult suffrage.

The political skills she acquired in this struggle she later applied tirelessly to other causes, such as the welfare of working mothers and their children. Her book **Save the Mothers** stressed the urgency for the provision of maternity welfare by the state. She wrote of the evil of fascism long before its dangers were apparent, addressed public meetings urging support for Ethiopia's struggle against Mussolini's fascist army. From 1934 onwards, Sylvia became increasingly involved with the anti-fascist movement in Africa, and devoted herself to the people of Ethiopia, living in Addis Ababa for the last five years of her life, a close friend of the Emperor Haile Selassie.

Sylvia's decision to work with the women of the East End caused considerable dismay in both her mother and her sister, Christabel. They were of the opinion that the East End movement was too working class and too democratic an organisation and therefore at odds with the ideals of the WSPU. "We want all our women to take their instructions and walk in step like an army!" Despite their objections, the East London Federation of the Suffragettes was formed on the 27 May 1913. Six months later, Sylvia was summoned to Paris, where Christabel had taken refuge to escape arrest, to be told that her East End organisation was no longer part of the WSPU. The now independent ELFS thrived as a grassroots organisation of socialist feminists. The onset of the First World War saw a radical change in the Suffragette movement. Emmeline Pankhurst called a halt to WSPU activities and gave her full support to the Government's war effort. The effect of this was to divide the movement and create the final split between Sylvia Pankhurst and the women who were revolutionary socialists and Emmeline and Christabel Pankhurst, Millicent Garrett Fawcett and the conservative feminists.

Sylvia Pankhurst lived in Bow for twelve years, and her life amongst the hardworking, often desperately poor women of the area is vividly described in her books, **The Suffragette Movement and The Home Front.** A third volume of autobiographical writing **In The Red Twilight** was drafted but never published. Many of the places associated with her work in the East End have disappeared, but a few have survived, and it is still possible to trace her life in Bow, and to walk in the footsteps of Sylvia Pankhurst and the East London Federation of the Suffragettes.

*Sylvia addressing the crowd at the opening of the shop in Bow Road*

# "Red Caps of Liberty"

*Committee Members of the East London Federation of the Suffragetttes. Their flag was the Purple, White and Green of the Suffragattes with the addition of "Red Caps of Liberty."*

When the Suffragettes decided to extend their campaign for women's right to vote into the East End of London, Sylvia Pankhurst and Zelie Emerson, her American friend, set out down the "dingy" Bow Road in search of premises. They found an old baker's shop, opposite St Mary's Church, and it was here that the first East London branch of the Women's Social and Political Union was set up in October 1912.

Sylvia Pankhurst recalls how she painted the board over the shop with the legend Votes for Women, gilding the letters "with true gold leaf," to the astonishment of the people of Bow. Norah Smyth took some striking photographs of Sylvia addressing the crowds from a wooden platform built with the generous help of Willie Lansbury, George Lansbury's eldest son. He supplied the timber from the Lansbury Wood Factory and helped out on many occasions. Willie lent his whole-hearted support to Sylvia's campaign, even to

the extent of going to prison for breaking a window. His wife Jessie was an enthusiastic Suffragette and was honorary secretary of the new branch.

In describing her feelings at the start of her East End Campaign, Sylvia Pankhurst wrote in **The Suffragette Movement**: "I regarded the rousing of the East End as of utmost importance .... The creation of a woman's movement in that great abyss of poverty would be a call and a rallying cry to the rise of similar movements in all parts of the country."

The women of the East End who heard Sylvia's rallying cry were those in the sweated trades, such as the bootmakers, brushmakers, matchmakers, as well as "ropemakers, waste-rubber cleaners, biscuit-packers, women who plucked chickens too often 'high', for canning, and those who made wooden seeds to put in raspberry jam."(**The Suffragette Movement**).

*Looking east down the Bow Road towards Stratford. The site of No. 198 midway is on the right*

At what was the junction of Bromley High Street with Devons Road, near the Rose and Crown pub, stood the Obelisk, "a mean looking monument" mentioned by Sylvia Pankhurst, in her book **The Suffragette Movement.** A postcard, dated 1911, (below) shows an ornate gas lantern above a drinking fountain beside a horse trough. It appears to form a traffic island close to C Selby and Sons, Undertakers (this shop moved to the Bow Road site in 1912.)

In February 1913 Sylvia stood on a cart placed against the wall of the LCC School and made her first momentous speech to the people of Bow. When the meeting passed without incident, Sylvia, in a desperate attempt to attract attention, threw a stone through the window of the undertaker's on the corner of Bow Road and Bromley High Street.

The sign on the derelict shop front was clearly visible, until recently. The entire row of shops was demolished in November 1990. St Mary's Court now occupies the site.

Mrs Watkins, Mrs Moore and Annie Lansbury were arrested along with Sylvia. Willie Lansbury smashed a window in the Bromley Public Hall, and Zelie Emerson broke a Liberal Club window. They were taken to Bow Police Station and charged. The East End Campaign had begun in earnest.

*View of the junction of High Street Bromley and Devons Road, c 1911, site of the Obelisk.*

Bromley by Bow Vestry Hall is built on the site of the Bowry Almshouses, a bequest from Mary Bowry, who died in 1715. In 1878 the almshouses were demolished and the Vestry Hall constructed.

The East London Federation of the Suffragettes held many of their meetings at the Bromley Public Hall, until they were debarred from holding meetings in Council Halls.

When Sylvia Pankhurst threw the stone which broke the undertaker's window, it was immediately followed by three more stones being thrown from amongst the crowd. Then Willie Lansbury ran out from the crowd, and with the cry of "Votes for Women," smashed a window of the Bromley Public Hall. Sylvia, Mrs Watkins, Mrs Moore, Annie Lansbury and her brother Willie were escorted to Bow Road Police Station and charged. Shortly afterwards, Zelie Emerson arrived, flushed with excitement, having broken the window of the Liberal Club in Bow Road.

Sylvia, Zelie and Willie were sentenced to two months hard labour. Annie, Mrs Moore, and

Mrs Watkins received a month each. Once in Holloway, Sylvia, Zelie and Mrs Watkins decided to go on a hunger strike. This was just the first of many more arrests and hunger strikes that the women were to undertake that year.

On Monday 27 July 1913, a meeting at Bromley Public Hall was broken up by the police, who attempted to arrest the suffragettes. Sylvia, Mrs Watkins and Mrs Ives hid in a nearby disused stable. At four in the morning Willie and Edgar Lansbury arrived with a wood cart. Sylvia was tied up in a sack and hidden under the piles of wood. She endured an uncomfortable ride in the jolting cart all the way to Woodford in Essex, where she was hidden in the home of the Lansburys' cousin Mrs Brine.

Annie Barnes, in her memoirs **Tough Annie**, describes Mrs Moore, who lived at 82 Turners Road, Bow, as being a "fine woman" and a "great friend of Sylvia's" who always carried a pomeranian dog with her when she went shopping. Annie, from Burdett Road, Poplar, and later Councillor for Stepney also describes her life-long friendship with Sylvia.

*Bromley Public Hall by floodlight*

In December 1913 Zelie Emerson, who had
organised a meeting at Bow Palace, a hall
close to the WPSU Office in Bow Road, led a
protest group to the home of the Conservative
Councillor John Le Manquais, Number 13
Tomlins Grove.  He was one of the
Councillors who voted against the Suffragettes
having the use of public halls, such as the
Bromley Public Hall, for meetings.  The group
numbering about two hundred were opposed
by about one hundred foot and mounted
police who attempted to dissuade them from
entering Tomlins Grove. When Zelie Emerson
stepped out to make a speech in front of Le
Manquais' house, the mounted police turned
their horses and charged the crowd.

*Zelie Emerson, 1914*

*Tomlins Grove, No. 13*

Several  papers including the Manchester
Guardian gave detailed accounts of this
incident.  The East London Advertiser gives a
vivid description of the scene:

*The shouts of police officers directing their men
to clear the streets were mingled with cries and
yells of women and children, who rushed here
and there to seek safety....Women and children
were thrown to the ground in the melee, many
being trampled on in the semi-darkness of the
narrow thoroughfare.*

Zelie Emerson sustained severe bruising and
had her arm in a sling when she appeared
before the magistrate, who discharged her,
saying she had suffered enough.  Police horses
are still kept in stables just across the road
from Tomlins Grove.

The Police Station is a rather elegant building erected in 1903 to replace the old building which was situated on the opposite side of the road, by the Bromley Public Hall. Part of the old Police Station can be seen at the rear of Massey's.

The Suffragettes, especially Sylvia Pankhurst, Zelie Emerson and Daisy Lansbury were frequent visitors to Bow Road Police Station during the years 1912 to 1916 as they resorted to violent methods in order to get arrested. To the rear of the building are the stables from where the mounted police rode out to quell the demonstrating women in Victoria Park.

The East London Advertiser recorded that excessive force was used by policemen, who usually resorted to charging the unarmed women and belabouring them with their truncheons. Women were often severely injured in these attacks. Plucky Zelie Emerson received blows to her skull on at least three occasions.

*Bow Road Police Station as it looks today*

She was beaten unconscious by a police truncheon in Victoria Park as a result of which she was forced to retire from suffrage activities for several months, and eventually returned to the United States.

*Mounted Police escorting a suffragette demonstration in the East End.*

The Minnie Lansbury Memorial Clock (above) over Electric House honours a remarkable woman. Minnie Lansbury (nee Glassman) was born in Stepney of Jewish parents, and was a school teacher until 1914, when she married Edgar Lansbury, son of George Lansbury.

Minnie was elected Alderman on Poplar's first Labour Council in 1919.  As Chairman of the War Pensions Committee, she became renowned for her efforts towards helping war widows and war wounded in their claims for financial assistance and pensions. The committee had the responsibility for five hundred war orphans in the Borough.

Minnie Lansbury joined the Workers' Suffrage Federation in 1915, and was assistant secretary from 1916, being re-elected in 1918 when the organisation changed its name to the Workers' Socialist Federation. Minnie shared Sylvia Pankhurst's socialist views, but she preferred to enter the mainstream of political life to fight for the rights of the workers. She and her husband Edgar joined the Communist Party in 1920. She was one of the five women on the Poplar Council who went to prison during the Poplar Rates dispute in September 1921.

The six week prison spell undermined her health, and she died of pneumonia a year later, at the young age of thirty-two. Her funeral from nearby Wellington Road was attended by thousands of mourners.

Nellie Cressall, long-serving Poplar councillor (elected Mayor in 1943) and a close friend, was among those who accompanied the funeral cortege down the Bow Road to the Jewish Cemetery in East Ham.

*Minnie Lansbury on her way to Holloway Prison, Monday 5 September 1921*

Edgar Lansbury, Minnie's husband, was a Labour councillor and later Mayor of Poplar, 1924-25. He and his brother Willie ran the family timber merchant business in Bow which was renamed the Russian Veneer Factory in 1921. There is an intriguing account of the part he played in the sale of the Russian Crown Jewels in London in 1920. The jewels were smuggled out of Russia by secret Soviet agents after the Russian revolution in 1916, and were hidden in the home of Minnie's parents Mr and Mrs Glassman, in Chicksand Street, a small turning off Brick Lane, Whitechapel.

Isaac Glassman, a coal dealer, arranged for their sale through a Hatton Garden merchant. The jewels fetched £40,000, and the money was intended to restore the flagging Daily Herald newspaper. The paper refused the money, however, and although questions were asked in Parliament, it is not clear what actually happened to the funds. Edgar later married Moyna McGill, a West End actress, and their daughter is Angela Lansbury, the American actress, who is proud of the fact that both her father and her grandfather served as Mayor of Poplar.

*The funeral cortege of Minnie Lansbury passes Bow Church on its way down Bow Road with her dear friend Nellie Cressall in attendance.*

*Memorial tablet on the site of Lansbury's home*

The Lansbury family lived at 39 Bow Road from about 1920. George and Elizabeth Lansbury dedicated their lives to the welfare of the people of Poplar, and both took an active role in the struggle for Women's Rights and the Suffragette Movement.

George Lansbury was elected to Parliament in 1910, as MP for Poplar, but resigned his seat in November 1912, and stood for election on the issue of Women's Suffrage. He was narrowly defeated, and did not re-enter the House until ten years later. During the intervening years he became Editor of the Daily Herald, through which he forcefully expressed his socialist and humanitarian views.

Elizabeth (Bessie) Lansbury bore twelve children, of whom three died young. All the Lansbury women were politically active, and the names of their daughters Daisie, Annie, Dolly (Dorothy), Violet, and daughters-in-law Jessie and Minnie crop up frequently in both Sylvia Pankhurst's accounts of the Suffragettes activities in the East End and in newspaper accounts of the period.

They were all arrested several times during the struggle for women's votes, and suffered

imprisonment and force-feeding. While Minnie's life was cut short, Jessie lived on to battle with spells of alcoholism. Daisy married Raymond Postgate and Dorothy married Ernest Thurtle. Both continued their political careers after their marriages, Dorothy being elected Mayor of Hackney, to her father's great delight.

When Bessie Lansbury died, Annie kept house for her father until his death in 1940. She later moved to Ilford, where she lived in sheltered accommodation. A year before she died she joined the Communist Party, as a result of which she suffered attacks on her home. Annie Lansbury died in 1952.

*George and Bessie Lansbury outside their home in Bow Road*

Built in 1849 by the Board of Guardians as a workhouse, the institution was converted in 1911 into an infirmary for "honest aged poor." In 1912, Julia Scurr, who had been elected to the Poplar Board of Guardians in 1907, wrote a report criticising the lack of amenities in the institution. She stated that as there was no common room, the inmates stood around in corridors, which were unheated; they were poorly clothed and the place conveyed a general air of depression. Her male colleagues on the Board dismissed the report as being exaggerated.

Julia Scurr was the daughter of John O'Sullivan, of Limehouse. She married John Scurr in 1900. Julia was a Poplar councillor from 1919-25. She served as a Guardian from 1907 until her death in 1927 and worked with George Lansbury and Sylvia Pankhurst organising several deputations. In July 1905 she headed a deputation of 1,000 women from Poplar to meet the then Prime Minister A J Balfour. In 1914 she led a party of six women suffragettes from Bow to meet Prime Minister

Herbert Asquith. They were: Mrs Watkins, Mrs Bird, Mrs Savoy, who had worked for forty-three years as a brushmaker and earned a penny farthing for a brush which took two hours to make; Mrs Payne who earned her living as a bootmaker and Daisy Parsons (later councillor and Mayor of West Ham 1936-37) who had worked since the age of twelve to support her mother and brothers, and now managed, on her husband's small wage, to care for her two little girls and an orphaned niece. This crucial meeting was the turning point in the suffragette's battle for the vote.

Both Julia and her husband John Scurr (MP for Mile End, Stepney 1923-32) had long careers in politics and worked actively for the Suffragette movement. They also supported pacifism during the 1914-18 war. In 1921 Julia Scurr went to prison along with her husband and fellow councillors from Poplar during the Poplar Rates Dispute. Her health deteriorated subsequently, although she remained a councillor until 1925, when ill-health forced her retirement. She died early in 1927.

*Three women Councillors of Poplar - Susan Lawrence, Julia Scurr and Jenny Mackay*

In October 1914 Sylvia Pankhurst, with the financial asistance of Norah Smyth, set up the East London Toy Factory at No. 45 Norman Road (now Grove) in an effort to provide work for East End women, and pay fair wages of not less than 5d an hour. Amy Browning, Edith Downing, Hilda Jeffries and a Miss Acheson designed and helped to produce the toys, the first batch of which were sold to Selfridges. The toys became so popular that other manufacturers copied the designs and undercut the market, which made it even more difficult for the factory to run at a profit.

The first toys were simple flat wooden animals, using wood from the Lansbury yard. Later soft toys were successfully produced, including dolls with porcelain faces. A factory catalogue shows the fine attention to detail which ensured the success of their sales, and also shows that dolls of all nationalities were made.

*45a  Norman Grove in 1991, looking west.*

*The  East London Toy Factory - making dolls for West End Stores*

The East London Toy Factory was set up to provide employment for East End women. Sylvia insisted that the workers were paid at a higher rate than that available in local factories.

The factory was managed by Mrs Regina Hercbergova, a Polish woman recommended by Keir Hardie. It was not a financial success, due in part to the high wages paid, and also to the alleged incompetence of Regina Hercbergova. This she vehemently denied, and threatened Sylvia with legal action when a statement to this effect was published in **The Home Front.** However, Norah Smyth was able to produce documents which showed that she had supported the project over the years through personal loans, which were never repaid.

Norah Veronica Lyle-Smyth, originally from Cheshire, was an accomplished painter and sculptor. She was also a keen photographer, and it is thanks to her that many of the suffragette activities in East London were recorded. In 1911 she took a studio in Chelsea where she met Sylvia Pankhurst. They toured Europe together in 1913, speaking on the suffrage movement.

On their return to Bow, they set up home at 400 Old Ford Road. Norah Smyth provided financial support for most of Sylvia's schemes, such as the **Woman's Dreadnought**, the Toy Factory and the Cost Price Restaurant. She had a gift for organising and practical planning. However, she had to sell her jewellery, her stocks and shares and even her furniture to keep the Toy Factory going. From being a wealthy woman, she became entirely destitute.

In 1924 she joined her brother Max in Italy, and worked for the British Institute. Around the same time Sylvia Pankhurst moved into the Red Cottage at Woodford Wells, Essex.

In 1931 Sylvia wrote to her asking for proof that she had made loans to the factory. Norah Smyth's response to Sylvia was very revealing, for not only did it show just how much money she had poured into Sylvia's projects, but she also remarked, "In 1922 you were thrown out of the committee!" Sylvia has not mentioned this in any of her writings. However, the date suggests that when Sylvia Pankhurst was sentenced to six months imprisonment for sedition towards the end of 1921, Regina Hercbergova gained control of the factory.

Norah Smyth died in Co. Donegal in 1963 at the age of eighty-nine.

The factory remained in business at Norman Road up to 1934, when it was relocated to King's Cross. Mrs Andrea Silk (nee Mead) of Bow, who began work at the factory in 1927, at the age of 14 years, still recalls the day she was asked to serve tea to Miss Pankhurst, who was paying them a visit.

Mrs Silk continued to work at the East London Toy Factory after her marriage, travelling to King's Cross from Bow. However, in 1943 business came to an abrupt end when the King's Cross area came under attack from German bombers. All the staff with the exception of Andrea Silk, who wanted to finish a piece of work, had adjourned to a nearby cafe for lunch. A bomb destroyed the cafe, killing most of the diners. The entire area was extensively damaged, and the factory was abandoned.

A nursery was opened in Norman Road as a creche for mothers working in the Toy Factory. The women could leave their children for the whole day at a cost of 3d which included food. The creche was soon full to capacity, and applicants had to be turned away.

Lady Sybil Smith, daughter of Lord Antrim, who was married to Vivian Hugh Smith (later Lord Bicester) helped to organise the creche and stocked the nursery with the toys discarded by her own seven children. Sylvia sadly recalled how Lady Sybil had presented them with a beautiful rocking horse, only to have it pulled to pieces by the little children of Bow, within a few days of its arrival.

Lady Sybil cheerfully supported Sylvia's activities in the East End, working at the creche four days a week, helping to relieve the suffering of children who were inevitably the first victims of the war. However, ill-health and the demands of her family forced her to curtail her activities. A Tolstoyan, she eventually drifted away from the ELFS, unable to accept their increasingly socialist views.

The need for a bigger establishment was soon apparent, and the "Mother's Arms" was opened in April 1915, at Old Ford Road.

*Lady Sybil Smith, left, in the garden at Norman Road with helpers and babies*

On the 13th October 1913 a meeting was held at Bow Baths Hall to welcome Sylvia and Norah Smyth on their return from Europe. Although the door was guarded against the police, they entered through the rear and sprang onto the stage wielding truncheons and sticks.

"Jump, Sylvia, jump!" yelled the crowd. She did so, and with a hat and coat to disguise her, she escaped. The others were not so fortunate. Mrs Ives was beaten with a truncheon and sustained a broken collar bone. Mary Leigh was knocked senseless; Mrs Forbes Robertson suffered a broken arm; Sister Townsend had her knee put out of joint.

*Sylvia Pankhurst, May 1913*

*Advertisement for Bow Baths, 1896*

Sylvia escaped into Lansbury's yard with the help of Willie Lansbury. The police, robbed of their prey and taunted with cries of "puss, puss" (a reference to the Cat and Mouse Act, and the celebrated poster showing a suffragette in the jaws of a giant cat) lashed out with their truncheons. Zelie Emerson, was once again struck by a police truncheon and knocked to the ground unconscious. The eminent surgeon Mr Mansell-Moullin of the London Hospital examined her and stated that had the blow struck a little further back, she would have been killed.

*The famous suffragette Cat and Mouse poster, depicting a suffragette "mouse" caught in the jaws of the government "cat"*

## "Spirits of the East End"

*The Pageant at Bow Baths Hall, January 1916:*

*Rear - Lily Gatward, the Spirit of Liberty and Joan Beauchamp, the Spirit of Peace. Joan later became the editor of the Conscientious Objectors' Tribunal, and served a term in prison as a result.*

*Centre - Mary Carr of Ranwell Street and beside her Violet Lansbury, the youngest of the Lansbury girls, garlanded with primroses as the Spirit of Spring. At each end are the Cohen sisters, dressed as lilies - Mary Cohen , on Violet's left, was Sylvia's secretary.*

*Front left - Rose Pengelly, the Spirit of the Woods plays the Pipes of Pan.*

*Kneeling in front are four little three-year olds, one at each end bearing the red caps of liberty, whilst the other two display the banners Peace and Plenty.*

Sylvia Pankhurst and her band of Suffragettes used the Bow Baths Hall regularly for their meetings and demonstrations. Bow Baths was a large complex containing a public laundry and slipper bath, besides a large hall for public meetings. It had an imposing frontage in Roman Road, facing Vernon Road.

On Thursday 6th January 1916 a New Year's party was held at the hall for 900 children. One of the young dancers was a young girl, Rose Pengelly. She was sixteen years old, a charming elf-like figure with green eyes, long red-gold hair - "a vision of loveliness," is how Sylvia describes her in **The Home Front**. She was nicknamed "Sylvia" by her workmates when she led them out on strike in July 1914 from Backs Asbestos Pipe Factory in Old Ford Road, into the Women's Hall nearby. She describes the work she was made to do in the 18 July 1914 issue of the **Woman's Dreadnought**. She packed the heavy "saggers of ware" and carried them to the furnace, ran errands for the housekeeper, peeled potatoes, and washed the "governor's" shirts and sheets!

The strike did not appear to have succeeded, for by August 1914, Rose was out of work.

Rose danced as the Spirit of the Woods in the New Year's Pageant and was the star of the show. She was scheduled to repeat her performance two days later. However, that Saturday morning, she caught her hand under the knife of a machine at work. Perhaps it was her excitement at the thought of the coming event, or just sheer exhaustion that caused her to have a lapse of concentration, we will never know.

Her new employer having refused her any help, Rose walked to Bow Station, took the train to the London Hospital, where, after waiting all day, the thumb and two fingers of her right hand were amputated.

The photograph of the Pageant reveals the obvious pleasure the children took in their performance, and the care that went into their costumes, although Sylvia does remark that the flimsy costumes often didn't completely hide their shabby, tattered under-clothing. These young girls worked long hours at arduous tasks and Rose Pengelly's tragic story only serves to underline the prevailing indifference most employers adopted towards their workers, who often worked a seven day week during the war years.

*Rose Pengelly (in white) with fellow strikers at 400 Old Ford Road.*

*People's Army: an organisation men and women may join in order to fight for freedom. And in order that they may fit themselves to cope with the brutality of Government servants.* (**The Suffragette Movement**)

Sylvia had planned to inaugurate her own People's Army at Bow Baths Hall on 5 November 1913. As she was liable to arrest under the Cat and Mouse Act, Daisy Lansbury, dressed as Sylvia, stepped out of the Lansbury house in St Stephen's Road and was swooped upon by the detectives, while Sylvia was hoisted over the wall into Willie Lansbury's house and emerged dressed as Daisy.

By the time the detectives had discovered their mistake, the meeting had got under way. Then Willie arrived at the Baths with the alarming news that a posse of three hundred mounted policemen were headed for the meeting. The crowd went out to meet them and in the ensuing struggle in the Roman Road, Zelie

Emerson was struck on the head by a uniformed constable, and fell to the ground unconscious.

Sylvia Pankhurst, however, escaped their clutches and hid in the Lansbury's house in nearby St Stephen's Road. Willie Lansbury once more packed her into a sack, covered her with piles of wood and drove her in a cart to the Rising Sun Inn, Woodford, where Norah Smyth was waiting with a car.

On 3 March 1914, Sylvia addressed a gathering of the People's Army from the window of 28 Ford Road. The recruits marched up and down Ford Road, with Norah Smyth at the head of the "Army" beating a drum. The police attempted to disperse the group, and in the ensuing struggle Norah Smyth, described on the chargesheet as "a sculptor, aged 34 years," was arrested on the charge of kicking a constable on the ankle, and striking another on the back of his neck with a drum stick.

*The People's Army training in Victoria Park.*

# "Down the Roman"

*The East London Federation of the Suffragettes selling the Woman's Dreadnought from their stall in the Roman Road*

*Site of 321 Roman Road*

Across the road from the junction of Roman Road with Parnell Road was the site of the second office of the East London Suffragettes, in what was a second hand clothes dealer's shop at 321 Roman Road.

As could be expected from the previous occupancy, the place was crawling with bed-bugs, and other unwelcome inhabitants, and despite their best efforts, the women were never able to fully eradicate them.

Mrs Watkins was installed as caretaker of the office. She was one of the first women to be arrested with Sylvia, in the Bow Road. She also undertook a hunger strike in February 1913, and was force-fed.

The Suffragettes sold the **Woman's Dreadnought** along the Roman Road. The newspaper was the brain-child of Zelie Emerson, who produced the pilot issue. The first edition appeared on 21 March 1914. Initial runs were in the region of 10,000, but later circulation dropped to around 1,000. Most of the articles were written by Sylvia herself, although other Suffragettes, notably

Melvina Walker, a docker's wife from Grundy Street, Poplar, wrote articles for the paper. Mrs Walker who had once been a ladies maid, was a fiery speaker, and regularly addressed meetings at Chrisp Street and Victoria Park. Silvio Corio, an Italian anti-fascist, contributed to the Christmas 1917 edition. He later took over the printing of the paper, and lived with Sylvia from 1926 onwards, although they never married.

In 1920 Sylvia employed a black journalist, writer and poet Claude McKay on a regular basis, while the popular journalist Henry Nevinson regularly contributed articles.

The ELFS also had a regular stall in the Roman Road where they sold home made produce, as well as the **Woman's Dreadnought**, to raise money for the Movement.

*Starting young.*

From June 1913 Sylvia Pankhurst was imprisoned ten times within a twelve month period. On each occasion she undertook a hunger and thirst strike. Released under the Cat and Mouse Act, her defiance of the ban on public appearances quickly led to her being re-arrested.

Both Mrs Payne and her husband were bootmakers by trade, but became closely involved with the Suffragette movement in the East End.  Their two children had both died, one in childhood, the other, who was mentally handicapped, at the age of twenty-seven. When 400 Old Ford Road was taken over and turned into the Women's Hall, Jessie Payne and her husband moved there with Sylvia Pankhurst. Mr Payne also organised a bootmaking scheme at  45 Norman Road, although from the accounts submitted, it  was not a financial success.

Jessie Payne was in the delegation of six working  women who went  to Downing Street to meet the Prime Minister, Herbert Asquith, on the 23rd June 1914.

*Sylvia Pankhurst  recovering at 28 Ford Road*

Jessie Payne lived with her husband at 28 Ford Road.  She was a dark-haired, pale woman of middle age, who was a devout  member of the Salvation Army in Old Ford.  She nursed Sylvia Pankhurst when she was released from Holloway, after the devastating experience of hunger, thirst and sleep strikes she underwent in prison.

*Sylvia Pankhurst and Jessie Payne with Keir Hardie's dog Bobby at No. 28 Ford Road*

In 1915 Sylvia Pankhurst was summoned to assist in the birth of what the Doctor gleefully referred to as "the first war baby! " **The Home Front** has a detailed account of the incident, which appeared to have affected Sylvia deeply. Although she gives us a wry and perhaps darkly humourous account of the event, it does reveal much of the prevailing social and moral attitudes of the era.

The unfortunate woman, who lived with her sister in Bow, suffered from a handicap, having been born with what was then referred to as a "club foot". She was also apparently extremely naive for she spiritedly denied being pregnant, claiming that what she had was simply a tumour. After being delivered of a son, she insisted she had no knowledge of how the pregnancy had occurred.

Weeks later the father, a soldier, appeared and reluctantly agreed to marry the mother of his child. Sylvia prevailed upon the Vicar to perform the ceremony, which duly took place, the bride on crutches, the bridegroom with a "ferrety look about the eyes," Mrs Fern holding a bouquet of flowers, and Nurse Hebbes carrying the baby. The Wedding Breakfast was held in the Women's Hall.

Sylvia later confessed that she had had her doubts as to whether she was in fact "committing a mortal sin in helping to tie the two together permanently." However, she also mentions that she spotted the reluctant bridegroom at a rally in Victoria Park, cheering the women on, so perhaps he was not such a bad lot after all.

*St Paul with St Stephen's Church, viewed from the north-west*

The Lansbury family lived at 103 St Stephen's Road, alongside the timber yard which was originally owned by Bessie Lansbury's father, Mr. Brine. It was from these premises that most of the Suffragette activities of Mrs Lansbury and her children took place. Bessie Lansbury joined the WSPU in 1906, and a year later Emmeline Pethick-Lawrence who founded the newspaper **Votes for Women**, along with her husband, wrote to Bessie thanking her for her support.

Willie Lansbury managed the timber yard and was later joined by Edgar his brother. They supplied the wood for the Toy Factory, as well as for the furniture for the Cost Price Restaurant and the Mother's Arms. The yard was renamed the Russian Veneer Factory around 1921, but the business later failed, and the brothers were declared bankrupt in 1926. Later Willie was to become a "hard-headed, hard drinking businessman", according to his son Terry.

*The Lansbury family help Sylvia and the suffragettes hoist the flag over 400 Old Ford Road. Sylvia is on the right, beside Jessie Lansbury who is holding her son, Terry.*

Sylvia Pankhurst set up the headquarters of East London Federation of the Suffragettes at 400 Old Ford Road. A roomy house which was once a private school, it was situated next to the Lord Morpeth pub, which is still in business, although the houses on either side of it have disappeared. A tree grows on the site of No. 400.

On 5 May 1914 with the help of the Lansbury family and an enthusiastic band of supporters, the flag of the East London Federation of the Suffragettes was hoisted on the roof of the building. The date was also Sylvia's 32nd birthday. On a sheet of ruled paper beginning with the words "We the Undersigned" sixty members and friends of the ELFS united in wishing her every happiness and success in the future and begged her to accept "a Dressing base as a small mark of our regard and esteem."

The large house was turned into a Women's Hall and later a Cost Price Restaurant was opened. The restaurant was run by Mrs Ennis Richmond, the gaunt, grey haired wife of a country clergyman, and her sister, Miss Morgan Brown.

The two sisters insisted on serving healthy, balanced and nutritious meals. In this they anticipated the present health food diets. However, some of the women who attended the restaurant protested at being made to eat "that muck" - potatoes served with their skins on, and plenty of dried beans. Meals cost as little as 2d, and could be eaten in the restaurant or taken away.

The house later served as the People's Russian Information Bureau, and regular weekly meetings were held in the hall until 1924, and were advertised in the **Workers' Dreadnought.**

*The Cost Price Restaurant, 400 Old Ford Road. Mrs Watkins, Mrs Farrell, Sylvia Pankhurst and Jessie Payne in the back row*

Mrs Savoy, a brushmaker by trade lived next door to the Lansbury's timber yard. Both Sylvia Pankhurst and George Lansbury have left glowing accounts of this short, rather stout woman to whom everyone turned for help. Despite her ailments - she suffered from "dropsy and palpitations," she adopted two boys who had been left orphans.

She was in the delegation of women who went to 10 Downing Street to meet the Prime Minister Herbert Asquith. She gave her name as Mrs Hughes, as her husband did not want his name associated with her suffragette activities. An elderly eccentric and a heavy drinker, whose brushmaking days were over, he was content to leave the work to his wife. Mrs Savoy's description of how she had earned her living for forty-three years making brushes, and the paltry wages she earned ,

shocked the Prime Minister. In November 1918 Mrs Savoy organised one of the first street parties for children to celebrate the end of the war.

Mrs Savoy died shortly after the end of the War. George Lansbury wrote a moving account of this neighbour of his who delighted him with gifts of beautifully made brushes, and his final comment, eloquently stated was: "...and one day the women of England will lead us out of the misery and degradation of slumdom and poverty, and will do so because millions of Mrs Savoys have shown by their lives that it can and will be done."

"The streets of Old Ford are colder and greyer with her loss," wrote Sylvia in tribute to one of her most faithful friends.

*Deputation of East End women to 10 Downing Street, 23 June 1914, photographed by Norah Smyth as they set off from 400 Old Ford Road. They are, from left to right:*
*Mrs Watkins, Mrs Jessie Payne, Mrs Savoy, Mrs Bird, Mrs Julia Scurr, Mrs Daisy Parsons.*

A disused pub, the **Gunmakers Arms**, located at 438 Old Ford Road, on the corner of St Stephen's Road and Old Ford Road, opposite Gunmakers Lane, was taken over by Sylvia Pankhurst, renamed the **Mother's Arms** and turned into a creche for working mothers. The letters ELFS were painted in gold on the outside surrounded by red caps of liberty. The creche was run by Lucy Burgis, a trained nurse. A regular clinic was staffed by two doctors, Alice Johnson and Barbara Tchaykovsky, a London County Council school doctor, and Nurse Maud Hebbes, who was later to become the first nurse at Marie Stopes' Birth Control Clinic. Lady Emily Lutyens, who was a follower of the Theosophical Movement headed by Annie Besant, sent one of her daughters there "to develop a social consciousness."

The creche attracted a great deal of publicity and public support, and as a result received grants from the City Corporation of London and the Ministry of Health and Education. Two years after the end of the Great War, the **Mother's Arms** finally closed its doors.

Barbara Tchaykovsky had earlier formed the Children's White Cross League to feed the

*Gunmaker's Lane, looking towards the site of the "Mother's Arms"*

dockers' children during the Dock Strike of 1912. Muriel Matters, just returned from studying under Maria Montessori in Barcelona, agreed to run a model school for the young children at the **Mother's Arms.** Once again, Willie Lansbury provided the wood for the furniture and shelves.

*Sylvia Pankhurst and one of her little charges, in the "Mother's Arms"*

Sylvia Pankhurst, Norah Smyth and Zelie Emerson were all involved in incidents in Victoria Park and at the Park gates. The Suffragettes held regular meetings in Victoria Park, where they sold the **Woman's Dreadnought,** later renamed the **Worker's Dreadnought.** Hannah Mitchell and Melvina Walker addressed meetings in the Park, amidst great disturbances.

On 24 May 1914, a Women's May Day in Victoria Park had been planned. Sylvia Pankhurst was escorted to the Park by a "chained guard" of twenty women, chained to each other and to Sylvia. On reaching the Park, they were apprehended by detectives dressed as costers, who bundled the women into the boating enclosure, and then proceeded to smash the padlocks on their chains. Sylvia reports, "Any woman who attempted to hinder the work had her face pinched, her hair pulled, arms twisted and thumbs bent back."

The Suffragettes' May Day processions attracted large crowds and much adverse

*May Day Procession along Old Ford Road, on its way to Victoria Park.*

publicity, and were invariably broken up by ruffians. Mounted police charged the crowds, often severely injuring the women. Zelie Emerson received a blow which fractured her skull, several women were reported to have suffered broken arms and severe bruising, and it says a great deal for their courage and the strength of their convictions that they were prepared to go out and face the violence yet again.

*Sylvia Pankhurst addressing a May Day Rally in Victoria Park*

On 27 May 1913, three days after the hugely successful May Day Procession, a meeting was held at Mrs Fischer's house, 304 Old Ford Road, to form the East London Federation of the local Women's Social and Political Union.

The minutes recorded the names of twelve women besides Sylvia Pankhurst. They were: Miss Fischer, Miss Elsa Dalglish, Miss Florence Haig, Miss Hicks, Mrs Leigh, Miss Brice, Mrs Walker, Mrs Ward Brown, Nurse Evans, Mrs Temple Bird, Mrs Ives and Lady Sybil Smith.

*(Below) Suffragettes in Victoria Park, 1916. Rose Pengelly is standing on the left.*

*(Above) Site of 304 Old Ford Road, at the corner of Grove Road*

A plaque marks the home of Israel Zangwill, poet, writer, and philanthropist, who lent his full support to Sylvia Pankhurst and the Suffragettes.

In December 1916, when he was asked to open the Women's Exhibition at Caxton Hall, Israel Zangwill ended his speech with the words "... the hope of the world lies in changing the **Gunmakers Arms** into the **Mother's Arms**. I trust that our Sylvia's action will be symbolic of the whole future course of history; for we will not pretend here that we are saving these babies merely that they may grow up to be food for cannon!"

*Israel Zangwill's house in Old Ford Road, with a commemorative plaque.*

*Norah Smyth's picture of the young children of Bow*

**October 1912**

Sylvia Pankhurst and Zelie Emerson, an American woman who joined the WSPU, (the suffrage organisation founded by Mrs Emmeline Pankhurst in 1903) and became an enthusiastic assistant to Sylvia, walk down the "dingy" Bow Road in East London, in search of a suitable office. They rent a baker's shop at 198 Bow Road for the Women's Social and Political Union. This marks the beginning of their East End Campaign.

**October/November 1912**

George Lansbury, Labour MP for Bow and Bromley, resigns his seat in Parliament. Stands for election on Women's Suffrage and is narrowly defeated. Sylvia begins to work with him in the East End.

**14 January 1913**

Sylvia leads a delegation of East London women to Lloyd George and Sir Edward Grey.

**7 February 1913**

WSPU open a shop at 321 Roman Road. Mrs Watkins installed as caretaker.

Meeting held in Bromley Public Hall, Bow. Sylvia, Zelie Emerson and Daisy Lansbury arrested for smashing a bank window in Bow. Released after Mrs Pankhurst pays fine.

**17 February 1913**

Sylvia Pankhurst addresses meeting at the Obelisk, "a mean looking monument in a dreary, almost unlighted open space near Bow Church". After meeting Sylvia flings a stone through the undertaker's window ( C Selby and Sons) and is arrested along with Annie and Willie Lansbury, Mrs Watkins, Mrs Moore and Zelie Emerson. All sentenced to two months hard labour. This, says Sylvia, marks the "beginning of the mass movement for Votes for Women in East London."

**10 April 1913**

George Lansbury arrested for protesting against Cat and Mouse Act. This notorious Act was passed in response to overwhelming public condemnation of forcible feeding of suffragettes on hunger and thirst strikes in prison.Under the Act hunger strikers are released to regain their health, then rearrested.

**11 April 1913**

Women's Suffrage meeting held in Poplar Town Hall. Councillors generally agree to support the cause.

**27 May 1913**

WSPU organises demonstration in Victoria Park along with other Labour organisations. Speakers Sylvia Pankhurst and Dr Letitia Fairfield have stones and bottles thrown at them. Ben Tillet and George Lansbury among speakers. Meeting breaks up in confusion, and the women gather in Mrs Fischer's house 304 Bow Road to organise an East London Federation of Suffragettes.

**June 1913**

Sylvia arrested and sent to Holloway. (In the next 12 months she is imprisoned 10 times, each time going on a hunger and thirst strike.)

**July 1913**

Sylvia brought from Holloway to Mrs Jessie Payne's house at 28 Ford Road. She stays here for several months, on each release from prison.

**13 October 1913**

Sylvia and Norah Smyth return from lengthy speaking tour of Copenhagen, Gothenburg, Norway, Budapest and Vienna to welcome in Bow Baths Hall. Detectives raid meeting. Women beaten mercilessly.

**5 November 1913**

People's Army inaugurated at Bow Baths Hall. Sylvia hides in Lansbury's house and escapes hidden in a wood cart.

**December 1913**

Zelie Emerson leads protest to Councillor John E Le Manquais house, 13 Tomlins Grove. The women and children are trapped by mounted policemen, 20 at each end of the Grove charge the protestors. Many women and children unable to escape are injured, including Zelie Emerson.

**3 January 1914**

Sylvia and Norah Smyth attempt to walk from Grove Road to Hackney, through Victoria Park. They are followed by detectives and arrested.

**27 January 1914**

East London Federation of the Suffragettes is founded after Sylvia travels to Paris at the request of her sister Christabel ,who informs her that her East London group are no longer part of the Women's Social and Political Union.

**8 March 1914**

First meeting of the ELFS at Trafalgar Square.

**14 March 1914**

Zelie Emerson works on producing a dummy copy of the Woman's Dreadnought, the name suggested by Mary Paterson. Sylvia notes she would have preferred The Worker's Mate - she liked the way people in the East End addressed each other as "Mate."

**21 March 1914**

First real edition of the Woman's Dreadnought appears. Initial runs are in the region of 10,000 which later drops to around 1,000. The paper is largely financed by Norah Smyth.

**22 March 1914**

Mothering Sunday march from Bow Bridge to Westminster Abbey. Daisy Parsons arrested for breach of the peace.

**5 May 1914**

Women's Hall opens at 400 Old Ford Road. The Lansbury family help Sylvia hoist the Suffragette flag on the roof. Sixty members and friends of the ELFS present Sylvia with a Dressing base "as a small mark of our regard and esteem" on the occasion of her thirty-second birthday.

**6 May 1914**

Zelie Emerson sails for America on the advice of her doctor.

# The Great War

**24 May 1914**

Women's May Day Procession held in East London, from Beckton via East India Dock Road, Chrisp Street, Fairfield Road and Old Ford Road to Victora Park. Sylvia Pankhurst waits at Women's Hall and is escorted to the Park in the centre of twenty women, chained to her and to each other. Detectives dressed as costers lie in wait to arrest the women, who are severely beaten in the process.

**18 June 1914**

Sylvia, weak from hunger and thirst strike, is carried in procession to Westminster. She crawls to the Strangers entrance and lies there until Prime Minister Herbert Asquith agrees to meet a delegation of East End women.

**23 June 1914**

Mrs Julia Scurr, Mrs Savoy (Mrs Hughes), Mrs Bird, Mrs Parsons, Mrs Watkins and Mrs Payne meet Prime Minister Asquith, who is moved by their testimonies of hard labour and appears to be impressed by their argument.

**14 July 1914**

Rose Pengelly leads the Strikers from Backs Asbestos Factory to the Women's Hall.

**4 August 1914**

Britain declares war on Germany, after the neutrality of Belgium ignored. The Great War begins.

**24 August 1914**

Cost Price Restaurant opens at 400 Old Ford Road. Mrs Ennis Richmond and Miss Morgan Brown manage the Restaurant on "health food" lines.

**17 October 1914**

Nursery and Boot Factory opens at No 45 Norman Road. Lady Sybil Smith in charge of Nursery. Mr Payne takes care of Bootmaking. Toy Factory also opens.

**February 1915**

League of Rights for Soldiers, and Sailors Wives and Relatives formed with George and Bessie

Lansbury, George Banks (Secretary of Poplar Trades Council) and Mrs H D Harben. Minnie Lansbury devotes her time working for the League of Rights. Sylvia hopes that this fusion of Labour and Trades Union with the Federation will bring them closer together.

**28 February 1915**

Lady Emily Lutyens speaks at Bow Baths Hall on "The Theosophic Ideal."

**April 1915**

Gunmakers Arms taken over and opened as the Mother's Arms, a Mother and Baby Clinic and Creche, with a Montessori School upstairs. Elizabeth (Bessie) Lansbury is made a Director of the Mother's Arms.

**13 April 1915**

Sylvia and Charlotte Drake lead a delegation to Board of Trade to demand equal pay for women.

**May 1915**

Sylvia, George Lansbury and Charlotte Drake meet Home Secretary Reginald McKenna to plead for price controls. When pressed for higher taxation on large incomes he says: "Rich people have their committments, they would be miserable if their incomes were greatly reduced." As they leave the meeting, McKenna, author of the notorious Cat and Mouse Act, stretches out his hand to Sylvia: "I must shake hands with you, you are the pluckiest girl I ever knew."

**26 September 1915**

Keir Hardie dies, broken in health and devastated by the war and the thought of worker pitted against worker. Sylvia deeply grieved at the loss of her friend. ELFS send wreath tied with their colours: purple for dignity, white for purity, green for young hope, and red for progress.

**6 January 1916**

New Year's Day Party at Bow Bath Halls for 900 children. Rose Pengelly aged 16 dances in pageant as the Spirit of the Woods.

**23 January 1916**

Anti-conscription meeting in Victoria Park. The speakers are Sylvia Pankhurst, Esther Roper, Eva Gore Booth, Charlotte Drake, Mrs Boyce and Miss Bouvier.

# Workers Suffrage Federation

**March 1916**

East London Federation of the Suffragettes change to Workers Suffrage Federation, to fight for universal suffrage. Minnie Lansbury elected secretary.

**8 April 1916**

Workers Suffrage Federation march from East End to a Rally against conscription in Trafalgar Square. Unruly mob hurl red and yellow ochre at women: Charlotte Drake's twelve year old daughter Ruby hit in face by packet of red ochre. Long-time supporters, such as Sybil Smith, withdraw their aid from Sylvia. Mrs Pankhurst disassociates herself publicly from her daughter's actions and policies.

**July 1916**

Charlotte Drake represents WSF at the British Dominions Women's Suffrage Union.

**August 1916**

Sylvia and Miriam Price lead a delegation of 20 Old Age Pensioners from Old Ford Road to the House of Commons to press for better allowances. Entertained by J M Hogge. Asquith agrees to concessions for pensioners in cases of real hardship.

**August 1916**

Sylvia Bailey, Sylvia's cousin, organises Festival of Children in Victoria Park. 60 children dance in a pageant.

**December 1916**

Womens Exhibition opens in Caxton Hall. Mrs Savoy has exhibition on various sweated industries, Mrs Drake demonstrates the effects of rising food prices and Muriel Matters runs a model Montessori class. Israel Zangwill opens the Exhibition.

**December 1916**

Demonstration for Peace at East India Dock Gates. Edgar and Minnie Lansbury arrested, along with Sylvia. Mrs Walker fined £2 for using insulting language. Mrs Drake arrested. All released.

# Votes for (some) Women

**December 1916**

Demonstration in Victoria Park. Crowd objects to call for peace as Melvina Walker speaks. Charlotte Drake and Nellie Cressall are thrown to the ground.

**February 1917**

Speakers' Conference publishes report. Recommends votes for all men over 21 and women over 30 who are University Graduates, owners of property, tenant householders or wives of the above.

From 1917 onwards Sylvia grows more involved with the communist movement, as do some of the other WSF members. However, some who do not approve drift away.

**1917**

Sylvia opens an orphanage for 30 children in Woodford, which she maintains for two and a half years.

**21 July 1917**

Last edition of the Woman's Dreadnought - paper renamed the Worker's Dreadnought.

**January 1918**

Representation of Peoples Bill granting limited suffrage to women. It takes another ten years before Parliament grants universal suffrage.

**May 1918**

Workers Suffrage Federation becomes Workers Socialist Federation, as Sylvia becomes attracted to the Communist Movement. However, she is sharply critical of Lenin and soon disenchanted with communism and its leaders.

**July 1918**

The People's Russian Information Bureau opens at Old Ford Road.

**October 1918**

Sylvia arrested and charged under the Defence of the Realm Act for causing disaffection amongst civilians and troops. Released after being fined.

**11 November 1918**

Armistice Day and the First World War comes to a close.

**November 1918**

Mrs Savoy organises Children's Peace Party in Bow, one of the first to do so to mark the Armistice and the end of the Great War. She dies shortly after the war and both George Lansbury and Sylvia are deeply affected by her departure. "The grey streets of Old Ford Road are greyer and colder for her loss," she writes.

**November 1920**

Sylvia Pankhurst sentenced to six months imprisonment in Holloway for sedition - "Six months for telling the truth." Norah Smyth organises processions to Holloway, and leads the singing of The Red Flag.

**1 September 1921**

Poplar Councillors arrested for refusing to levy rates in the Borough. George Lansbury, leads the Councillors and Aldermen, among them five women, into direct confrontation with the Government. They are all sentenced to a term of imprisonment dependent upon them paying the arrears.

**5 September 1921**

Women Councillors and Aldermen, Susan Lawrence, Julia Scurr, Nellie Cressall, Minnie Lansbury and Jennie Mackay arrested. A crowd of 10,000 escorts them down East India Dock Road to Holloway. All the women, with the exception of Susan Lawrence, are active in the East London Federation of the Suffragettes. Nellie Cressall, mother of five and six months pregnant, is released after sixteen days. The others spend six weeks in prison.

**1 January 1922**

Minnie Lansbury dies at her home, 6 Wellington Road, aged thirty-two.

**27 April 1922**

Sylvia Pankhurst "thrown out of the toy factory committee" after disagreement with Mrs Hercbergova. (Norah Smyth's letter to Sylvia 1931, when she supplied evidence of continued financial support to the factory.)

**May 1924**

Sylvia moves to Red Cottage in Woodford with Silvio Corio. Stepney councillor Annie Barnes and her husband maintain a close relationship with her. Norah Smyth leaves to settle in Italy.

**June 1924**

Workers Dreadnought closes down after Sylvia refuses to hand over control of the paper to the British Communist Party.

**December 1927**

Sylvia Pankhurst, aged 45, gives birth to the son she so longed for - Richard Pankhurst. Causes a great scandal when she publicly announces his birth, as well as the fact that she does not intend to marry the father of her child - Silvio Corio. Devotes herself to motherhood and writing.

**14 June 1928**

Mrs Emmeline Pankhurst dies, as the Bill for universal suffrage receives its final reading in Parliament. The Bill is passed in July.

*The Red Cottage, Woodford Wells.*

# Select Bibliography

The Suffragette Movement - E Sylvia Pankhurst (Virago Press Ltd 1977)

The Home Front - E Sylvia Pankhurst (The Cresset Library 1987)

Sylvia and Christabel Pankhurst - Barbara Castle (Penguin Books 1987)

Votes for Women - Diane Atkinson (Cambridge University Press 1988)

Suffragettes - Diane Atkinson (Museum of London 1988)

Shoulder to Shoulder - Midge Mackenzie ( Penguin Books 1975)

Tough Annie - Annie Barnes (Stepney Books 1980)

Poplarism 1919-1925 - Noreen Branson (Lawrence and Wishart 1979)

Good Old George - The life of George Lansbury - Bob Holman (Lion Publishing plc 1990)

Fly a Flag for Poplar - Geoff Richman 1975

Deeds not Words, The Lives of Suffragette Teachers - Hilda Kean (Pluto Press 1990)

Hidden from History - Sheila Rowbotham (Pluto Press 1973)

Discovering Women's History - Deidre Beddoe (Pandora Press 1983)

Stepping Stones to Women's Liberty - Les Garner (Heinemann 1984)

Women on the Warpath - David Mitchell (Jonathan Cape 1965)

Rise Up Women - Andrew Rosen (Routledge and Kegan Paul 1974)

Sylvia Pankhurst, Artist and Crusader - Richard Pankhurst (1979)

Portrait of a Radical - Patricia W Romero (Yale University Press 1987)

Sylvia Pankhurst in Perspective (Some comments on Patricia Romero's biography) - Rita Pankhurst (Women's Studies Int. Forum Vol 11 No. 3 1988) by Rita Pankhurst.
Note: It is advisable to check Rita Pankhurst's paper, a copy of which is in the Fawcett Library, which details inconsistencies in Patricia Romero's book.

The Local History Library at Bancroft Road, Mile End, London, has an extensive collection of books on East London, as well as maps, newspaper clippings and photographs. The Reference Library at Stratford has an interesting collection of suffragette memorabilia.
The International Instituut voor Sociale Geschiedenis, Amsterdam, has the complete collection of the manuscripts, papers and photographs, as well as many sketches and paintings of Sylvia Pankhurst, a gift from her son Richard Pankhurst.

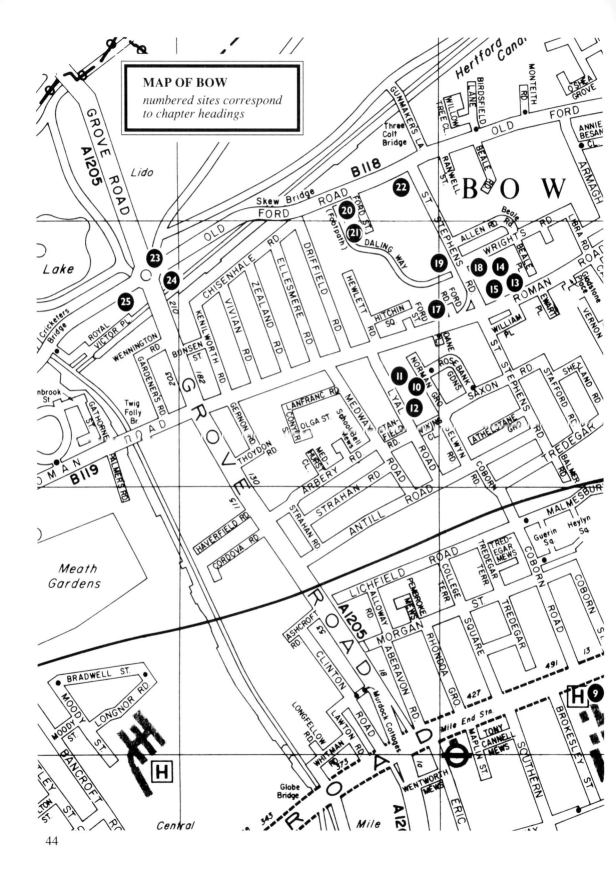

**MAP OF BOW**
*numbered sites correspond
to chapter headings*

44

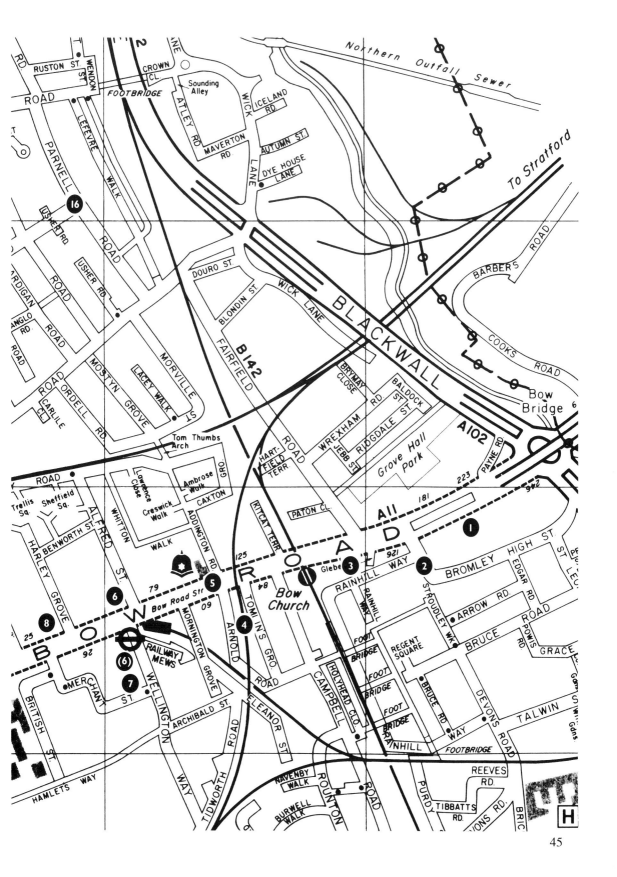

Other publications from Stepney Books

## MY POPLAR EASTENDERS

*by Carrie Lumsden. £4.95, illustrated.*
Insight into life as a child in Poplar during the First World War.
0 9505241 7 4

## EDITH AND STEPNEY

*by Bertha Sokoloff. £4.95, illustrated.*
The life of Edith Ramsay. Education, politics and social change in Stepney
1920-79.
0 9505241 6 6

## MEMORIES OF OLD POPLAR

*by John Blake. £1.20, illustrated.*
Poplar family and street life between the Wars.
0 9505241 1 5

## CHILDREN OF THE GREEN

*by Doris M Bailey, £3.95, illustrated with line drawings.*
Cheerful autobiographical portrait of Bethnal Green family and street life
between the Wars.
0 9505241 4 X

*All the above books can be ordered from:*
*Stepney Books Publications, 19 Tomlins Grove, London E3 4NX.*

*Postage extra on small orders. Usual trade terms.*

*Stepney Books Publications is a community publishing group producing East End
history and autobiography.*